Searchlight
BOOKS™

Animal
Superpowers

Exploding Ants

and Other Amazing Defenses

Rebecca E. Hirsch

Lerner Publications ◆ Minneapolis

Lerner Publications Company
A division of Lerner Publishing Group, Inc.
241 First Avenue North
Minneapolis, MN 55401 USA

For reading levels and more information, look up this title
at www.lernerbooks.com.

Library of Congress Cataloging-in-Publication Data

Names: Hirsch, Rebecca E., author.
Title: Exploding ants and other amazing defenses / Rebecca E. Hirsch.
Description: Minneapolis : Lerner Publications, [2016] | Series: Searchlight Books.
   Animal Superpowers | Audience: Ages 8–11. | Audience: Grades 4 to 6. | Includes
   bibliographical references and index.
Identifiers: LCCN 2016010957 (print) | LCCN 2016012730 (ebook) | ISBN
   9781512425444 (lb : alk. paper) | ISBN 9781512428193 (eb pdf)
Subjects: LCSH: Animal defenses—Juvenile literature. | Adaptation (Biology)—Juvenile
   literature.
Classification: LCC QL759 .H57 2016 (print) | LCC QL759 (ebook) | DDC 591.47—dc23

LC record available at https://lccn.loc.gov/2016010957

Manufactured in the United States of America
1-41312-23256-5/24/2016

Contents

Chapter 1

SLIMY HAGFISHES

Animals have many ways to defend themselves against predators. Some run. Some hide. Some fight back with sharp teeth and claws. And some use unusual strategies to protect themselves. The hagfish relies on gooey, slippery slime.

Hagfishes, also called slime eels, are nearly blind. How do hagfishes find their way?

A hagfish lives in a burrow on the bottom of cold ocean waters. It slithers like a snake along the seabed. The hagfish is nearly blind, but it has a good sense of touch and smell. It feels its way around and finds food with a ring of tentacles around its mouth. It smells with a single nostril on the top of its head. It eats small invertebrates or carcasses that settle to the ocean floor. A hagfish seems defenseless. But its body is ready for an attack.

Hagfishes can go months without eating. They can absorb nutrients through their skin and gills.

SHARKS AND OTHER FISH ARE A HAGFISH'S MAIN PREDATORS.

As the hagfish feeds on a fish carcass, it does not notice a shark swimming along the bottom of the ocean. The shark swims closer, watching the hagfish. To the shark, the hagfish looks like easy prey. The shark moves quickly. It grabs the hagfish in its jaws and tries to bite down. It doesn't know that the hagfish's body is armed with a unique weapon.

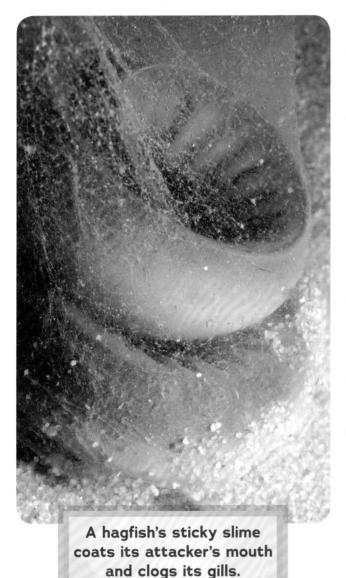

A hagfish's sticky slime coats its attacker's mouth and clogs its gills.

Slime Attack

Snot-like slime oozes out of the hagfish's body. Instead of a meal, the shark gets a mouthful of slime. Choking, the shark drops the hagfish. The shark gags, trying to remove the slime from its mouth and gills. Meanwhile, the hagfish has escaped. The shark will not attack this creature again.

What just happened? Hagfishes have large slime glands inside their bodies. They have about two hundred slime pores running the length of their bodies. When attacked, they release slippery goo through their pores. The slippery stuff expands in seawater to form thick, sticky slime. The slime fills the mouth and gills of an attacker.

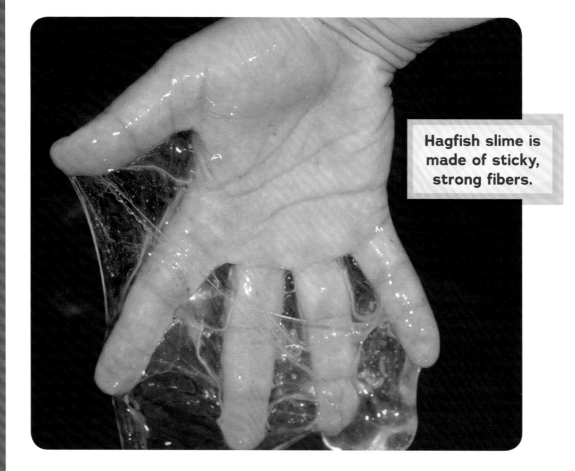

Hagfish slime is made of sticky, strong fibers.

Compare It!

Like hagfishes, fulmar chicks defend themselves by launching something gross at their attacker. Fulmars build their nests high on rocky cliffs. The parents must leave the chicks behind when they go out to fish at sea. All alone in their nests, the chicks are easy prey for gulls and other birds. When a predator approaches, fulmar chicks vomit fishy stomach oil at it. The oil not only stinks, but it also coats the feathers. The sticky feathers are no longer able to keep birds dry and warm. Predators hit by the smelly, sticky vomit can later die from chilling or drowning.

Fulmar vomit can be deadly to other birds.

Eating dead animals on the ocean floor makes the hagfish part of an ocean's cleanup crew!

Hagfish slime has other uses too. When a hagfish eats, a small amount of slime oozes out of its pores. A group of hagfishes sometimes feeds together on a carcass. They produce a cloud of slime. The milky cloud keeps other animals from joining the feast. That means more food for the hagfishes.

Keeping Clean

Sometimes the hagfish gets slime on its own body. To get rid of the sticky mess, the hagfish ties its tail in a knot. Then it slides its body through the knot. This action scrapes its body clean.

A hagfish might also sneeze to clear slime out of its nostril.

Chapter 2

EXPLODING ANTS

A predator that attacks the Malaysian carpenter ant may be in for a nasty shock. These ants live in rain forests in Asia. Fierce weaver ants live there too. Carpenter ants are under constant attack from weaver ants in battles over territory. The carpenter ants are no match for weaver ants in a fight, but they have a surprising weapon.

Carpenter ants live in the rain forest. What other kind of ants live there too?

Malaysian carpenter ants' bodies are packed with poison. Large glands filled with poison run from their jaws to the tip of their abdomens. When an ant is attacked, either by an enemy ant or a predator, it runs. If the attacker doesn't go away, the ant turns and faces its enemy.

Weaver ants are one of the main enemies of Malaysian carpenter ants.

Suicide Mission

The ant contracts its abdomen. Pressure builds up inside the ant's body. Then, like an over-filled water balloon, the ant's body explodes. Poison bursts out of its mouth and the tip of its abdomen. Poison blasts through its exoskeleton, the hard shell that protects its body.

This carpenter ant explodes to protect its colony.

SOME PREDATORS MAY BE ABLE TO
SURVIVE A CARPENTER ANT'S ATTACK.

The sticky poison sprays all over its attacker. The poison sticks to its legs and jaws. The exploding ant dies in the attack. Sometimes the attacker dies too. But if it survives, it learns not to disturb this kind of ant again.

These blue-spotted termites may die to protect their colony from attack.

Scientists call this defense tactic autothysis. This word comes from the Greek words for *self* and *sacrifice*. The ant sacrifices itself for the good of the colony. Malaysian carpenter ants aren't the only insects to use autothysis. Some species of termites also blow themselves up in defense.

Compare It!

The sea cucumber is another animal that fights with its guts. When a fish swims up to take a bite, the sea cucumber contracts its muscles. Its intestines, stomach, and other organs burst out through its rear end. While the fish tries to avoid getting tangled in the sticky stuff, the sea cucumber creeps away. Unlike the exploding ant, the sea cucumber lives on. In about six weeks, it regrows its lost body parts.

A sea cucumber's insides can be toxic to other fish.

Chapter 3

ARMORED PANGOLINS

A pangolin walks across dry ground on its back legs, sniffing the air for ants. With its scaly body, the pangolin can be mistaken for a reptile. But this mammal's scales are made of fused hairs. The pangolin finds a likely spot to dig. It rips into the earth with its powerful claws. Ants swarm out of the hole. The pangolin slurps them up with its long, sticky tongue.

The pangolin is a mammal with a body covered in scales. What are the scales made of?

Unnoticed by the pangolin, a lion is hiding in the grass. The lion's muscles tense. It leaps at the pangolin. But the pangolin curls into a ball. The lion tries to grab hold of it, but the lion can't get a grip on it. The lion bats the pangolin around like a soccer ball. Finally, the curled-up pangolin starts to give off a stinky smell. The lion has had enough. It moves on.

Lions, leopards, and hyenas are all predators of the pangolin.

Pangolins often walk on just their back legs because their claws are so big.

A Scaly Mammal

Many predators lurk in the African grasslands where pangolins live. Pangolins are slow-moving creatures. So they can't run away from other animals. They are not ferocious fighters. They don't even have teeth! Pangolins do have huge claws, but they mainly use them for digging up ants and termites, not for fighting.

Armored Stinkball

The pangolin is well-protected against predators. It wears a full armor of overlapping scales. The scales cover most of its body, except its underbelly and face. When threatened, the pangolin curls into a tight ball, which is very hard for predators to grab. It wraps its scaly tail around its body and hides its soft underbelly, face, and limbs safely inside.

Pangolin **means
"something that rolls up."**

Compare It!

The armadillo lizard also rolls into an armored ball to defend itself. Spiny scales cover its body too, and its soft underside is not armored. If a predator such as a hawk ambushes the lizard, it rolls itself into a ball and bites its tail, hiding its soft belly inside the ball. In this pose, the lizard is a spiny mouthful that is almost impossible to swallow.

This lizard has rolled itself into a spiny ball so it won't be eaten.

The pangolin's scales are razor-sharp. If a predator does manage to get hold of the scales, the pangolin can contract its muscles. Anything trapped between the scales is shredded. The pangolin can stay in a ball for hours as it waits for the predator to go away. The pangolin might even roll down a hill to escape. If all else fails, the pangolin oozes a stinky fluid from a gland near its tail. The smell is bad enough to keep predators away.

Chapter 4

BURROWING OWLS

A bobcat trots through a field. It spies a hole in the ground. It crouches by the hole, ready to pounce. From inside the hole comes a rattle. It sounds like a rattlesnake. But it is the sound of a burrowing owl chick. The bobcat jumps back. It looks elsewhere for its meal.

Burrowing owls live in dry areas of Central, South, and North America. Where do they nest?

Burrowing owls live underground in burrows that have been dug out by ground squirrels or prairie dogs. The problem with nesting on the ground, rather than high in a tree, is that many predators roam around. Snakes, hawks, falcons, coyotes, skunks, badgers, dogs, bobcats, and house cats all may enter the burrow and eat young owls.

This burrowing owl sits in front of its underground burrow.

If the adult owls can stand guard outside the burrows, the chicks are safe. But sometimes the parents must go out hunting for lizards, mice, and frogs. They leave the chicks in the burrow alone. With so many predators roaming around, the young burrowing owls are very vulnerable.

Nesting on the ground puts burrowing owls at risk of attack.

Playing Tricks

When the parents are hunting, the owl chicks stay out of sight inside the burrow. If an unwanted visitor comes, the chicks give off a cry of alarm. Their cry is a long, rattling hiss. The hiss sounds like the warning rattle of a dangerous rattlesnake.

These chicks spend much of their time underground.

Rattlesnakes are another animal that sometimes lives in a burrow.

Many predators know that rattlesnakes sometimes curl up inside prairie dog burrows. Rattlesnakes rattle their tails as a warning before they bite. Burrowing owl chicks unconsciously mimic, or copy, the sound of a rattlesnake. Predators hear what they think is a venomous snake curled up inside the hole. Experienced predators steer clear.

The burrowing owl chick's call is an example of mimicry. The chick wards off predators by imitating a dangerous animal. The deception works because the chick remains hidden. Scientists have discovered that the burrowing owl's sound is very effective. In one experiment, ground squirrels were nearly as alarmed by the owl's hiss as they were by the sound of a real rattlesnake.

SCIENTISTS BELIEVE THAT MANY PREDATORS ARE SCARED OFF BY THE OWL'S HISS.

▼

Compare It!

The Virginia opossum also uses trickery to stay safe. When threatened by a predator, this furry animal plays dead. It flops on its side and lies motionless. Its tongue hangs out, and spit gurgles from its mouth. Then it lets out a stinky, green slime. The slime smells like a rotting corpse. Most predators won't eat an animal that's already dead, so they give up and leave the opossum alone.

This Virginia opossum pretends to be dead so predators don't come near.

Chapter 5

HORNED LIZARDS

A fierce-looking lizard calmly chews ants. This odd creature is a horned lizard. It has horns on its head and spines along its body. This spiny armor protects the lizard by making it hard for predators to see—and even harder to swallow.

Horned lizards live in deserts. How do their spines protect them?

Despite getting a spiny mouthful, coyotes, bobcats, roadrunners, owls, and snakes all attack horned lizards. But the lizard has tricks it can use. The lizard can hiss and inflate, or puff up, its body to twice its normal size, making it look like a spiny balloon. This makes the lizard seem bigger than it really is and can scare away a predator.

Horned lizards have a few different ways to keep predators away.

The Evil Eye

If nothing else works, horned lizards have a unique and effective weapon. They shoot blood from their eyes! When a predator approaches, the lizards allow blood pressure to build in their head. The blood bursts out of ducts in the corners of their eyes. The horned lizard can squirt blood at a predator 3 feet (1 meter) away.

Horned lizards will shoot blood at only a few kinds of predators.

Compare It!

A bombardier beetle also squirts a nasty poison at its enemies. The beetle shoots a jet of boiling-hot, poisonous spray from its rear end. Inside the beetle's abdomen are two special glands with thick walls. Each gland holds a different mix of chemicals. Kept in their own compartments, the chemicals aren't hot or toxic. But when the beetle is attacked, the glands open and their contents mix together. The mix is toxic, smelly, and as hot as boiling water. Predators don't stand a chance.

The bombardier beetle can aim its toxic spray left, right, under its body, or over its head.

The blood confuses the attacker and gives the horned lizard a chance to get away. The squirting blood also contains a chemical that tastes bad to coyotes, dogs, and wolves. If these predators get squirted by a horned lizard, they quickly learn never to mess with this well-armed creature.

A horned lizard's blood tastes especially bad to coyotes and other dogs.

Animals have amazing superpowers to stay safe from their enemies. They might launch a slime attack, wield razor-sharp armor, shoot blood, or even blow themselves up! Some of these superpowers can seem pretty strange. But they all help animals in the battle for survival.

How else do you think animals might defend themselves?

Extinct Animal Superpowers

- *Ankylosaurus* has been called a living tank. This school-bus-sized dinosaur spent its days munching grass, protected by heavy armor on its body. *Ankylosaurus* also had a heavy, clubbed tail that it could use to whack its attackers.

- *Triceratops horridus* was a dinosaur with three horns and a shield-like plate on its head. *Triceratops* was a plant eater and may have used its horns to charge predators such as *Tyrannosaurus rex*. The bony plate may have protected its neck from predators.

- *Doedicurus* was a South American mammal about the size and shape of a Volkswagen Beetle. This slow-moving creature was protected with a thick shell of armor on its body and a clubbed, spiked tail. *Doedicurus* went extinct about eleven thousand years ago.

Glossary

burrow: a hole in the ground made by an animal

contract: to make something smaller or shorter

exoskeleton: a hard shell on the outside of the body

intestine: a long tube that is part of the digestive system

invertebrate: an animal that lacks a backbone, such as a clam or snail

mimicry: the resemblance of one living thing to another that gives it protection from predators

predator: an animal that kills and eats other animals

prey: an animal that is hunted and killed for food

seabed: the floor of a sea or ocean

tentacle: a long flexible arm of an animal, used for moving or grabbing

territory: an area that is occupied and defended by a group of animals

vulnerable: at risk of attack

Learn More about Animal Defenses

Books

Cusick, Dawn. *Get the Scoop on Animal Snot, Spit & Slime! From Snake Venom to Fish Slime, 251 Cool Facts about Mucus, Saliva & More.* Morganville, NJ: Moondance Press, 2016. Check out this book to discover more fascinating facts about the science of animal fluids.

Johnson, Rebecca L. *When Lunch Fights Back: Wickedly Clever Animal Defenses.* Minneapolis: Millbrook Press, 2015. Meet more animals that are amazingly good at self-defense.

Whitfield, Phil. *Attack and Defense: Astonishing Animals, Bizarre Behavior.* New York: Kingfisher, 2011. Learn more about the many ways animals protect themselves from attack—and about the animals attacking them.

Websites

ARKive
http://www.arkive.org
This site from the wildlife group Wildscreen features photos, video, and audio clips of many animals and includes information about how they survive.

Discovery
http://www.discovery.com/tv-shows/other-shows/videos/nasty-by -nature-hag-fish-slime
In this video, watch a scientist get slimed by a hagfish and learn more about this amazing animal.

National Geographic
http://channel.nationalgeographic.com/wild/worlds-weirdest/videos /blood-shooting-eyes
Learn about the amazing defenses of the horned lizard in this video, and see it squirt blood out of its eyes.

Index

Photo Acknowledgments

The images in this book are used with the permission of: © blickwinkel/Alamy, pp. 4, 26; © Mark Conlin/Alamy, p. 5; © Greg Amptman/Shutterstock.com, p. 6; © Brandon Cole, pp. 7, 8; © Jouan Rius/Minden Pictures/naturepl.com, p. 9; © Emory Kristof/National Geographic/Getty Images, p. 10; © Tom McHugh/Getty Images, p. 11; © Up Close with Nature/Getty Images, p. 12; © Visuals Unlimited, Inc/Tan Chuan Yean/Getty Images, p. 13; © Mark Moffett/Minden Pictures, p. 14; © Piotr Naskrecki/Minden Pictures, p. 15; © Dr. Robert Hanus, p. 16; © Kjell B. Sandved/Science Source/Getty Images, p. 17; © Natural History Media/Alamy, p. 18; © Frederick Mark Sheridan-Johnson/Alamy, p. 19; © Suzi Eszterhas/Minden Pictures, p. 20; © Images of Africa/Alamy, p. 21; © Nature Picture Library/Alamy, p. 22; © Mint Images/Frans Lanting/Getty Images, p. 23; © M. Timothy O'Keefe/Alamy, p. 24; © Arco Images GmbH/Alamy, p. 25; © All Canada Photos/Alamy, p. 27; © iStockphoto.com/johnaudrey, p. 28; © All Canada Photos/Alamy, p. 29; © David M. Schleser/Science Source/Getty Images, p. 30; © Design Pics Inc/Alamy, p. 31; © John Cancalosi/Alamy, p. 32; © Raymond Mendez/Animals Animals, p. 33; © Satoshi Kuribayashi/Minden Pictures, p. 34; © kojihirano/Shutterstock.com, p. 35; © Rod Patterson/Getty Images, p. 36.

Front cover: © Mark Moffett/Minden Pictures.

Main body text set in Adrianna Regular 14/20.
Typeface provided by Chank.

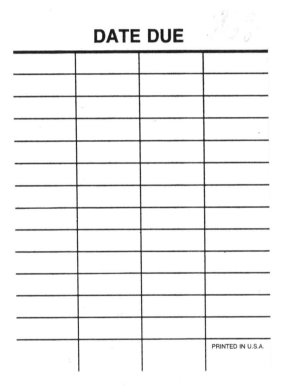

DATE DUE

PRINTED IN U.S.A.